THE BROKEN HEARTS MANUAL

WALL OF LOVE, BOOK 1

GEORGE ANTHONY MARCHIANDO, POET

Published & Distributed by:
George A. Marchiando

in association with;
IBJ Book Publishing
41 East Washington St., Suite 200
Indianapolis, IN 46204
www.ibjbp.com

Library of Congress: 2014955744
ISBN: 978-1-939550-14-9
First Edition
Printed in the United States of America

DEDICATION

The Broken Hearts Manual
is dedicated to everybody who has a broken heart.

I dedicate my poems to my wife.
Theresa Marchiando, my soulmate. I appreciate the way
that she keeps me coming back
to reality when I'm gone.

Pray for anything,
and if you have faith you will receive it.

LIVING HERE LIKE YOU'RE NOT MINE

Breaking away,
making up the days as they started.

Looking through the glass,
till the pain comes once back around.

And my sun is the same,
as it became when all the clouds have parted.

I'm filled with sunlight,
that never makes a flickering sound.

Running far, far behind me,
all of love's hours spent in a hard way.

Living here like you're not mine,
was there something I wanted from you today?

Long is the day as you wake up from the darkness;
long is the day that echoed deep into the night.

Living alone,
living here like you're not mine.

Was there something you wanted from me today,
breaking away?

NEVER WOULD HAVE GONE AWAY

I think about you all the time,
while I write the words that rhyme.
Just what I am thinking,
all these thoughts I'd love to say.

If it were up to me,
I never would have gone away.

Thought these California canyons
would have set me free,
but with the blue sky
there's no blue eyes staring back at me.
Just what I am thinking,
all these thoughts I'd love to say.
If it were up to me, I never would have gone away.

And for just that one moment,
your eyes are all I see.
Knowing that you're so far away from me.

And there's plenty of time for me
to find where I went wrong.
Tell me you want me back and I'll go home,
right back where I started from.

More than anyone else could find,
I realize what I want from you this time.
And that's you standing right before my eyes.

And if there never comes another time for me to say,
then I'll see your eyes in the blue California sky.

ALL THE RIGHT WORDS TO SAY

I try to think of all the right
words to say,

But deep inside, I know you
have gone away.

So I try to write
things I thought about you last night.

Then I stray away.

Don't lose that thought,
save it for another day.

You're everything I feel deep inside;
you're everything I wrote down last night.

So I'll try once again,
to sit down with paper and pen,

And try to write.

Don't lose that thought,
save it for another night.

NO ONE TO WRITE TO

I have my broken heart
I hold my little poems in.

Still got my mind
with a picture of you.

And I have my arms so I can write
these poems when I'm feeling blue.

Got my memory always reminding me,
you're no longer by my side.

I have my soul that I gave you,
that neither one of us can find.

Got my hands to wipe my eyes,
sometimes I want to die.

But if I did,
I would have no one to write to.

And when I am through
with this poem to you,

I'll still be alone.

I have my broken heart,
I hold my little poems in.

Still got my mind
with a picture of you.

SOMEHOW YOU'RE STILL MINE

Awakening to the alarm sound,
don't think I can fight this anymore.

Because I realize now,
that you won't be standing at my door.

Then I'll close my eyes for a little while,
remembering your face, remembering your smile.

And maybe someday I'll find,
that somehow you're still mine.

But through all this heartache,
when I close my eyes, you never go away.

No matter what I say,
or how much I write,
it's not better since you have gone away.

Does the ending really matter,
now that I have got you in my heart?

And awakening to the alarm sound,
that is when all of this starts.

Then I'll close my eyes for a little while,
remembering your face, remembering your smile.

And maybe someday I'll find,
that somehow you're still mine.

ISN'T LOVE STRANGE,
JUST WORDS PREARRANGED?

Does my love for you seem strange,
all these words I prearrange?

Some I wrote before,
could I have thought of anymore?

With every word I'm closer to say,
what your love meant to me today.

Was it lost in the back of my mind,
for me to bring it up another time?

Sometimes I just wish I could be in your eyes,
to reflect what it is I feel inside.

Just to be a thought in your mind,
looking back, where I was, when you were mine.

Does my love for you seem strange,
all these words I prearrange?

And with every breath that I breathe,
still it will be you that I'll need.

With what makes up my days,
with what makes up my nights.

Makes me want to hang my head and cry.
Wish I could be in your heart, to be one in your life.

Wish I could be in your arms,
looking back where I was, when you were mine.

Isn't love strange,
just words prearranged?

I'VE GONE AWAY

The sky was dark and, grey,
leaving out on a winter's day.

Though the fire, it keeps me warm,
in my mind I've gone away.

And my love feels more lively,
when I dream you're beside me.

My love flows freely.
When you need me, I've gone away.

I set off before the dawn,
before your memory has begun.

Now I'm feeling your warmth on my face,
with the morning sun.

And my love feels more lively, when I dream you're beside me.
My love flows freely.
When you need me, I've gone away.

The mornings I've spent alone,
with skies of darkened grey.

All I need is for you to tell me you love me so,
and make it all go away.

And my love feels more lively,
when I dream you're beside me.

My love flows freely.
When you need me, I've gone away.

COLORS OF RUSTLING SOUND

I walked out into the autumn day,
and stared at the dead leaves upon the ground.

And the breeze it played me a melody,
with the colors of rustling sound.

I thought how we both have become strangers.
Was I a fool to laugh with you through the summer sun?

What was the reason I wasn't the one?

Now I'm alone, you have gone,
why do I keep thinking these thoughts about you?

Why does my heart have to recall,
when all I wanted was to take you along?

Time's just a season,
thought I was strong.

When I add it all up,
the tears and the heartaches flow.

With every ounce of energy,
I can't seem to let you go.

And the autumn takes the summer,
and the winter takes the autumn.

And on, and on it goes,
with the colors of rustling sound,
from dead leaves upon the ground.

REMEMBER BACK THEN

Do you remember back then,
when we were just friends?

Never wanted the day to end,
planned when we would see each other again.

The days were long; we had our favorite song.
Thought nothing could ever go wrong.

Do you remember back then?

When we fell in love, we held hands,
and drew hearts on our skin.

You said this is our new start,
swore we would never part,
now that I got you in my heart.

Do you remember back then?

When you went away,
the silence I heard
meant you had nothing more to say.

Got to find the way to bring back yesterday,
and fall in love again.

Do you remember back then?

When I was always on your mind,
laying with you by my side,
we drew hearts on our skin.

How I thought our love
should have risen above,
now that we're just friends.

Do you remember back then?

MY LOVER'S PRAYER

Don't think there will be any loving for me tonight,
when I don't have you here by my side.

No blowing kisses to you in the air,
no flirting with your long stares.

No fancy dresses will lie on the floor,
here will be no love letters slipped under my door.

No I love you's will be whispered today,
now that you have gone away.

I'll feel no arms holding me tight,
off and on up into the night.

Won't see the eyes I desperately need to see,
won't hear the voice, I need calling for me.

No hand to wear a wedding ring,
no one to be my everything.

Only memories I'll forever hold tight,
as I lay down my heart tonight.

Giving me his lover's prayer,
that God will give me a world with you there.

THE POEM

x xxxxx xx xxxx xxxx xxxxxxxxx,

xx xxxxx xxx xxx xxxxx xxxxx xx xxxxx.

xxx xx xxxxxxxx xxx xxx xxx xxxxxx xx xxxx xxx.

xxx xxxx'x xx.

xxxxxxx xxx x xxx xxx xxx xxx xxxxxxx xxx.

x xxxx xxxxxx xxxxx xxxxx xxxxx xxx,

xxxx xxxx xxxxx xx xxxxx xx xxxx xx xxx.

xxxxxxxxx xxxx x xxxx xx xxx xxxx x xxxxxx xxx xx,

xxxx xxx xxxx xx xx xxx xxxxxxxxx xx xxxxx xxx.

THE SEQUEL OF THE POEM

I dream so very hard sometimes,
to write you all these words to rhyme.
All my memories now are all rolled up into one.

But that's ok.
Because now I have you and the morning sun.

I will always write poems about you;
your love gives my heart so much to say.

Beginning with a poem of how much I miss you so,
when you wake up at the beginning of every day.

ALL ALONE AGAIN TONIGHT

I'm all alone again tonight.
I shouldn't be dreaming,
should have been to sleep by now.
And the loneliness doesn't make a sound.
I'm all alone again tonight.

So go ahead and close your eyes.
Your heart has been through so much pain,
you should be dead by now.
Until sleep can hold me tight,
I'm all alone again tonight.

Is there a place here in my bed,
safe enough to lay down my heart and head?
No, the feeling just isn't right,
I'm all alone again tonight.

Somewhere you will close your eyes,
and somewhere else I'll close mine.
And loneliness doesn't make a sound,
I'm all alone again tonight.

As I lie here all alone,
me and the silence,
should have thought of a way by now.
Instead of dreaming of holding you tight,
I'm all alone again tonight.

A POET'S TEARS

A poet's tears cannot be heard,
for he keeps it inside to be put down in words.

He can be warm as the sun,
or as cold as the snow.

For his soul only travels,
anywhere a peaceful wind may blow.

There's a mysterious way,
that he walks into a room.

He's one of life's finest actors,
when he hides all his gloom.

All of his memories,
the good and the bad.

Have about taken all the love,
that his heart ever had.

But yet the ones that still care,
are at the top of his list.

He wants to put down into words,
the things in life they might have missed.

Though he is silent,
he's never ending.

His mind will rest nevermore,
going back to the little things that made his heart soar.

A poet's tears cannot be heard
except from God above.

For his hopes and dreams and prayers are to be held
in the arms of true love.

MORNING BREEZE BLEW THROUGH MY MIND

The morning breeze started softly
through the curtains.

Then waved them high,
as it rattled pictures that hung on the wall.

Danced with the clothes that lined my closet,
then shut the door before it wandered down the hall.

With not a creak from the stairway,
down the banister it flew.

With the sweet smell of flowers,
and the freshness of morning dew.

Carried the smell of coffee brewing,
out of the kitchen and across the living room floor.

Rippling through the pages of an open book,
that's scattering sunlight on the bathroom door.

It caresses the cat then hides behind
the contour of the couch and chair.

And I feel just a little less alone,
when it seems like you are somewhere downstairs.

Like a child running and playing,
I hear the empty beer cans roll when they fall.

And up the stairs carried out on the breeze,
the sound of your voice would call.

Then suddenly the dream was over,
with the window slamming hard;
the breeze and sound fell.

Then everything in my room was quiet,
and once again stood still.

Taking my memory back was easy,
before the winds of change came through.

The way my heart would float on air,
and follow you through every room.

SHARE WITH ME

Share with me, the robin sings,
at the start of morning light.

Lift me up, my spirit soars,
as clouds go passing by.

But touch me softly now summer breeze,
because you could be this day's only delight.

For my heart rushes along the day,
for the peace sleep brings at night.

Share with me, the robin sings,
as the sun moves through the sky.

It's plain to see that you loved her so,
for it's standing the test of time.

But come and watch and hear me sing,
don't let the day's colors fade from your sight.

You seem to hold her in some lost world,
until sleep can hold you tight.

Share with me, the robin sings,
as the sun starts to fall from the sky.

A thousand times I called for you,
but I guess you didn't know why.

A thousand times I sent in the breeze,
to see if you were alright.

I've tried everything in this world,
I guess it's now up to the night.

With passing sound now silent,
as the robin wings up to his nest.

I said yes my friend, I know you tried,
as my heart slipped off to rest.

MUCH CALMER NOW

Much calmer now,
bullet hit its mark,
and I came tumbling down.

Much calmer now,
as I float six feet off the ground.

Much calmer now,
just six feet away from family and friends,
and they can't hear what I say.

Much calmer now,
as they make their last sounds.

Much calmer now,
six feet of dirt separates me from
the ones I love.

Much calmer now,
as their tears hit the ground.

WHEN OUR SMILES TOUCH

See how our hands come together,
feel the softness when our smiles touch.

Keep me walking in your shadow,
never comes the day without you, I see.

Echo all the days with our laughter,
never comes the night not spent with you.

And if it ever comes to ever after,
make sure you take me with you.

See how our hands come together,
feel the softness when our smiles touch.

Keep yourself walking in my shadow,
and keep ever closer to our love.

Never comes the day without you, I see,
never comes the night not spent with you.

If this is our last day together,
make sure you take me with you.

LOVE'S DYING SEED

Well it came to be on one spring day,
the love that I felt when you came my way.

You wanted me, you told me so,
and said with love like a seed,
we'll watch it grow.

The summer brought laughter
of days spent in the sun,
and the breeze carried our promises
that we would always be one.

Our nights filled with magic
from a moon that hung so low;
my arms like vines I'd hold you,
my heart like a root grabbed hold.

For fall now brings its beauty,
like your smile I stand back to behold.
The magic in the swirling leaves,
the deep blue sky that seemed so bold.

I thought our love would last forever,
and I took for granted the things you need.
Like the daily care and love I'd give,
when our love was just a seed.

Came the change of the seasons,
came a big change in you,
and as cold as winter wind,
your words cut right through.

Now the harvest is done,
and snow covers the leaves,
and all that's left standing,
is a man planted in grief.

He keeps thinking back,
of a fertile spring day.
Wondering if the seed of love
could ever again grow
in his heart,
now hard as clay.

LIFE GETS IN THE WAY

Dear mother, she was one of a kind,
her love was something that was hard to find.

Always keeping us boys right in line,
to a mother like her, it was the best of times.

Father he worked hard everyday,
just so his boys could stay home and play.

It seems we always got in a fight,
now that I'm older I know that he was right.

To my son that I hold dear,
I'd walk a thousand miles just to have you near.

Wish that there was something we could do today,
but you know how life always gets in the way.

I finally found a girl to be my wife,
now everyday in love we live our life.

Wish it would never end; wish we never got old.
I hope in death I'll have her hand to hold.

This is the story of my life,
day to day, sometimes I don't get by.

Seems like I had a lot more to say.

But you know how life always
gets in the way.

I GUESS ALL YOU REALLY OWN
IS THIS LETTER FROM HOME

My dear son, the day is coming soon
when you leave prison and I can touch you.
When they give you back to me
all the flowers will have bloomed.

When you are released it will just be me and you.
I hope this love in my letter, finds you son.
A letter is all I can do.
It's been so lonely here since you have been gone.
Everything has been the same old thing around here now.
I'm just missing you, and I'll write my love for you.
I guess all you really own is this letter from home.

I'm sorry I haven't written so much,
but everyday I have felt your love,
one more day I keep holding on. Sending my son
a letter from home.

Now you can read it out loud or show everybody,
like you're not locked up with all your buddies.
You're not scared late at night when you wake up,
and find that you have no one to hold you tight.
I guess all you really own is this letter from home.

You'll probably keep it in your shirt.
Then pull it back out, re-read the words.
Everyone looks away when a prisoner finally
breaks down and cries.
And while no one's looking he'll just wipe his eyes.
Just one more day he keeps holding on.
All over a simple letter from home.

ESCAPING LOVE

Dark and dusty night of love,
filled with stars that shine above.

Moon covered over with night of a blue
wind shattering dust that showers our view.

Through tarmac and never ending,
cry of tears when love dies.

His mind traveling through hell,
for glimpses of her and a sunny sky,
and all he can ask is why.

Through sultry days,
He awaits the breeze.

As it chases the heat,
through the top of the trees.

The smell of each field as it blows into one,
the beauty of each ray that comes from the sun.

And he sits and wonders,
with never-ending tears.

As love speeds away from him,
year after year.

GREATEST SHOW I EVER KNEW

Love is a tightrope way up high,
there is no net and you can't fly.

All you can hope for is that she'll hold on tight,
as I inch my way to the other side.

Just like the crowd you left in the night,
in my dressing room I'm still holding you tight.

The greatest show on earth I ever knew,
was when I held you.

Circus life, just another show,
it's what all the smiling faces don't know.

And as the clowns try to make me smile,
I think of you with every passing mile.

Every night I look for you in the crowd,
and just before I hit the ground.

The greatest show on earth I ever knew,
was when I held you.

I AWAKE TO THE SUNSHINE

I awake to the sunshine,
To the sunrise,
In the morning time.

Just as my world crashes down.

I thought you would forever be mine,
In the sunshine,
For a long time,
But I guess you left me now.

In the sunshine.

The sun was in her eyes.
Daylight told me the night is over.
Guess she waited for the right time,
When she said in the sunshine,

This is really goodbye,
For a long time.

Is this how my mornings begin
And end?
Is this what I don't love you
Feels like?
Now it's too late to begin again,
In my life,
Today,
Anyway.

I awake to the sunshine,
to the sunrise,
in the morning time,
Just as my old world crashes down.

I thought you would forever
Be mine,
In the sunshine,
For a long time,
But I guess you left me now.

I awake to the sunshine.

THE LAST DAYS ON EARTH

She hasn't been feeling well lately,
and I sensed something was wrong.
Never dreamed I would have this story to tell,
that was unlike any other love song.
They think she has cancer.

You know we didn't sleep very well that night.
And my heart grew heavy,
as I saw the fear in her eyes.
You see I was the man
who had all the right words to say;
The one who made everything alright.

And all I could say
was that I would soon be with her,
and she wouldn't be alone for very long,
until once again I'd hold her tight.

You should never break the heart of a poet.
For he will surely die a slow and painful death,
if he dies of a broken heart.

As another tear appears
out of the corner of her eye,
I slowly turns to my wife.
And as I hold her tightly,
and stare into her deep blue eyes,
my poet's heart starts to speak,
and this is what my heart had to say.

I DECIDED TO LET GO

The day has finally come.
There's no more wishes I can make.
And all these memories are more than I can take.
There are no more solutions.

Although I thought of another one,
I'll search for you somewhere beyond the sun.

I held on tightly to this world
because of you and the love you have given me.

But now the Lord has taken that out of my control
and I think the world would forgive me
if I decided to just let go.

No, I never saw it coming.
Seems like you just came and went.
And I know my time on earth will come to an end,
just so I can see you again.

There's another day coming,
when we will be together again,
because a love like ours,
will never end.

I held on tightly to this world
because of you and the love you have given me.

But the Lord has taken it out of my control
and I think the world would forgive me
if I decided to just let go.

Yes, I made a decision
with no chance to make another one,
that I'll go looking for you
somewhere beyond the sun.

I held on tightly to this world
because of you and the love you have given me.

But the Lord has taken it out of my control
and I think the world would forgive me
if I decided to just let go.

THE ONLY MAN LEFT IN THIS WORLD

In my whole life I find that I
never saw anything more beautiful to me,
except for you.

This new life that I have now,
isn't what I thought life would be,
this world is not for me.

The days aren't getting any better,
and the nights are getting way too lonely.

Your dying made me feel like
I'm the only man left in this world.

Watching my family cry for me,
now I think that they can see,
that I just can't take this feeling of being alone.

There's no more rhythm and rhyme in me,
I just can't seem to get over you,
even if I wanted to.

The days aren't getting any better,
and the nights are getting way too lonely.
Your dying made me feel like
I'm the only man left in this world.

I'm still looking for your face,
and nothing can take your place for me,
being alone.

The days aren't getting any better,
and the nights are getting way too lonely.

Soon I will be with you.
I can't live
like I'm the only man left in this world.

MY BROKEN HEART

And the story kind of goes like this.

Once upon a time,
in a not too distant land.

Tucked safely away highly within
the fortress of her castle walls.

She was guarded by the magic
of Merlin the Wizard,
a thousand horses,
and a thousand brave and loyal knights.

They were all dressed in armor and white satin,
waiting for her royal call.

Here once lived
a very, very beautiful queen.

And you know how you always made me feel
like I was your king.

And we would live happily ever after,
so the story goes.

And the story goes on, and on, and on,
round, and round, and round.

Like a fairy tale,
they were so deeply in love.

But then suddenly the story ended.

57

THE SEQUEL OF MY BROKEN HEART

One day God came to take
the beautiful queen back to his kingdom.

But the king loved the queen so much
that he wouldn't let God take her away.
So he called on the magic of Merlin the Wizard.

Merlin said "God's got more power than me,
although I've got just enough magic
to give you and the queen one more day."

But the king loved the queen so much,
that he turned to God to say,
"I will fight you God with all I have,
I will not settle for just one more day."

So he told his knights about the queen
and they very much loved her, too.

So the knights prepared for battle
and waited on the queen's royal call.
Because without the queen and her love,
there would be no kingdom at all.

Then the wizard rushed in to see the king
to tell him what he saw in his crystal ball.
He said, "An army of angels is gathering
outside of the castle walls."

And the king and knights loved her so much,
that they ordered the drawbridge to drop and fall.
Because without the queen and her love,
there would be no kingdom at all.

And with their blades drawn,
out went 200 brave knights,
and when they reached full gallop,
the king charged out 200 more.
And when they reached full gallop,
the king sent out 200 more.
And the king watched 600 knights
that had no fear at all.
Love is the greatest thing
that God ever created.

And the knights were very brave,
and they loved her so much,
that they would give up their lives
for their beautiful queen.
Because without the queen and her love,
there would be no kingdom at all.
So wave, by wave, by wave,
the brave knights,
they hit the angels hard.
The sound of swords and armor clanged,
then horses and knights would fly through the air and fall.
And all the knight's white satin turned to red.

Then the king turned to his beautiful queen,
as his tears started to fall.

Then the queen made a demand,
"I cannot let another brave knight fight and die for me.
I love you, too, and my heart would break
if I was to lose you all.

Because without my knights and their love,
there would be no kingdom at all."

Then the queen started to cry,

but the knights never saw their beautiful queen cry before.

She was always happy and they always felt her love.

And they all knew in their hearts,

that she would soon be gone,

no more love,

no kingdom at all.

Then the last 400 of her bravest knights,

with tears in their eyes,

and their hearts started to break,

they disobeyed the royal call.

They charged out bravely with their swords drawn,

ready to die for their love.

Because without the queen and her love,

there would be no kingdom at all.

And when they reached full gallop,

400 brave knights hit the angels hard.

The sound of swords and armor clanged,

as horses and knights started to fly through the air and fall.

And all the knight's white satin

turned to red.

Then God took the queen away,
and to the king God said,
"I know you have a broken heart.

And I've never seen a greater love,
where men would rather be dead
than to lose their queen and her love."

A thousand brave knights and a beautiful queen
are now in heaven up above.

God said, "People call me the King,
because I created you and love.
And when I come for your broken heart,
you and your queen will meet up above.

You will help me rule my kingdom.
You and she will always be my King and Queen of Love;"
because without God and His love,
there will be no kingdom at all.

BIRTHDAY POEM

Well hello there again,
wonder if you're really my friend.

Because each time I'm closer to death.

But the time in between,
told or unseen,
always try to make it your best.

Your __ year might shed you a tear,
but remember the best is yet to come.

You'll find out things
like the beauty love brings,
so share yours with everyone.

And when next year rolls around,
bring one thing to mind.

The mistakes you have found,
can only work out in time.

Happy Birthday I'll say to a
special __ that I know.

I'll throw in I love you,
and my how you're getting old.

ABOUT THE AUTHOR

George Anthony Marchiando was born in Indianapolis on April 27, 1958. He lived his early years over his parent's honky tonk bar which he accredits to his dear love of music today. He grew up on the hill of the Spring Hill Motel and enjoyed what he believed a nearly perfect life with excellent parents, a race car and a motorcycle. He considered himself a "cool" guy.

George was an All Star football player at Cascade High School until a teacher saw a beer can in his car. He had to miss his high school homecoming and became bitter with life in general. He met his son's mother and traded scholarships from some of the finest schools to have his son. He feels he made the right decision because the love of his son is far greater than being a pro football player. His first wife left him on their anniversary.

Many dreams resulted in a number of career pursuits. George tried to start a daredevil show, but he could not find financial supporters. Now he hopes to have the proceeds from this book of poems to allow him to start that stunt show.

George made a deal with the Lord. It is said that for every dollar you donate to God, God will give you back tenfold. The projects George hopes to accomplish are renovating a large building where previous prisoners would have a job and home until they get back onto their feet. Also, he would like to renovate property to house kennels for animals belonging to people who do not have money or a home to care for them. In addition, he would like to have property to house the homeless. By starting these businesses, he would be creating jobs for those in need so they are not dependent on the government.

George stopped working with his heavy construction job. He now has time to write. This is Book One of his poetry and he has 10 more poetry books to come. Publishing his award-winning poetry has been a life-long wish.